Firefighter

by **Dana Meachen Rau**

Reading Consultant: Nanci R. Vargus, Ed.D.

Marshall Cavendish
Benchmark
New York

Picture Words

 ax

 boots

 fire

firefighter

 fire truck

 helmet

 hose

 ladder

3

A 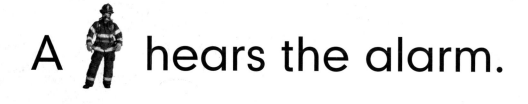 hears the alarm.

A  puts on .

A  puts on a .

A 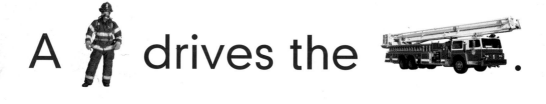 drives the .

10

A  holds the .

A  uses an ⚒.

A climbs a .

A sprays the water.

A  puts out a .

Words to Know

alarm
   a warning sound

climbs (klimes)
   to go up

drives
   moves or goes from place to place

helmet
   a hard hat that protects your head

Find Out More

Books

Bridges, Sarah. *I Drive a Fire Engine*. Minneapolis, MN: Picture Window Books, 2006.

Gordon, Sharon. *What's Inside a Fire Truck?* Tarrytown, NY: Marshall Cavendish, 2004.

Kalman, Bobbie. *Firefighters to the Rescue!* New York: Crabtree Publishing Company, 2004.

Minden, Cecilia. *Firefighters*. Chanhassen, MN: Child's World, 2006.

Schmidt, Erin. *What Does a Firefighter Do?* Berkeley Heights, NJ: Enslow Elementary, 2005.

Videos

There Goes a Fire Truck. Kid Vision.

Popular Mechanics for Kids: Firefighters and Other Life Saving Heroes. Koch Vision, 2006.

Web Sites

Sparky the Fire Dog
http://www.sparky.org/
U.S. Fire Administration for Kids
http://www.usfa.dhs.gov/kids/flash.shtm

About the Author

Dana Meachen Rau is an author, editor, and illustrator. A graduate of Trinity College in Hartford, Connecticut, she has written more than two hundred books for children, including nonfiction, biographies, early readers, and historical fiction. She lives with her family in Burlington, Connecticut.

About the Reading Consultant

Nanci R. Vargus, Ed.D., wants all children to enjoy reading. She used to teach first grade. Now she works at the University of Indianapolis. Nanci helps young people become teachers.

Marshall Cavendish Benchmark
99 White Plains Road
Tarrytown, NY 10591-9001
www.marshallcavendish.us

Library of Congress Cataloging-in-Publication Data

Rau, Dana Meachen, 1971–
Firefighter / by Dana Meachen Rau.
     p. cm. — (Benchmark rebus)
Summary: "Easy to read text with rebuses explores the job of a firefighter"—Provided by publisher.
Includes bibliographical references.
ISBN 978-0-7614-2617-2
1. Fire extinction—Juvenile literature. 2. Fire fighters—Juvenile literature. 3. Rebuses—Juvenile literature. I. Title. II. Series.
TH9148.R38 2007
628.9'25—dc22
2006036854

Editor: Christine Florie
Publisher: Michelle Bisson
Art Director: Anahid Hamparian
Series Designer: Virginia Pope

Photo research by Connie Gardner

Rebus images, with the exception of boots and hose, provided courtesy of Dorling Kindersley.

Cover photo by Robert Llewellyn/SuperStock

The photographs in this book are used with the permission and through the courtesy of:
PhotoEdit: p. 2 Lon C. Diehl (boots); Getty: p. 3 Karen Block (hose); Corbis: p. 5 Creasource; p. 11 Robert Landau; p. 13 Richard Hutchings; p. 15 Jim Zuckerman; PhotoEdit: p. 7 Richard Hutchings; p. 21 Spencer Grant; Getty: p. 9 Plush Studios; The Image Works: p. 17 Lisa Krantz; p. 19 Steve Warmowski.

Printed in Malaysia
1 3 5 6 4 2